A 3-minute forever book

EAT YOUR PEAS®

Faithfully

By Cheryl Karpen

D0961716

To _____

from _____

At the heart of this little book
is a promise.

It's a promise from
me to you
and it goes like this:

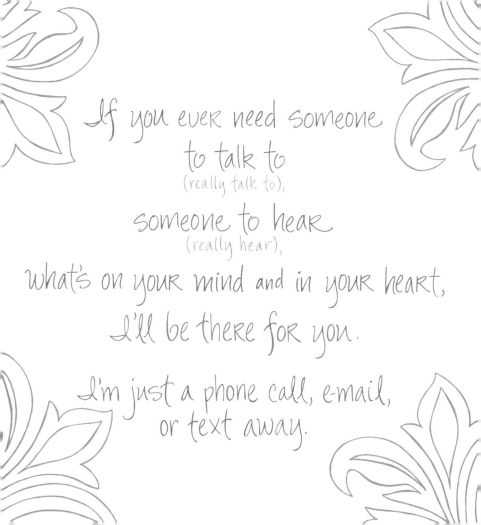

If you ever need someone
to talk to
(really talk to),

someone to hear
(really hear),

what's on your mind and in your heart,

I'll be there for you.

I'm just a phone call, e-mail,
or text away.

I promise to listen to you

with all my heart,
faithfully
and confidentially.

What's more, I promise to
cherish you,
lift you up and, if I can
help it, never, ever let you down.

In the meantime,
here are a few things
I'd like you
to know,
remember,
and never, ever doubt:

God loves you
in
extraordinary
ways!

Unconditionally, with grace, mercy,
and compassion, God's love for you is real.

Are any of us flawless? Of course not.
But that doesn't lessen God's love for us.
We are imperfectly perfect.

God's love is infinite.

Thanks be to God for his indescribable gift!
2 CORINTHIANS 9:15 NIV

You
make the
world
a better place.

When you have faith in one person, it changes a life.

When you have faith in yourself, it changes you.

When you have faith in God, it changes the world.

My faith in you is boundless!

When God created you in His magnificence,

He created a masterpiece.

There is nobody else quite like you. Nope.
Not anywhere. Not among all the six billion people
who live on this earth. Your eyes, nose, fingers,
heart, and mind are uniquely yours.

Undoubtedly, God is the best artist of them all.

*You made all the delicate, inner parts of my
body and knit me together in my mother's womb.
Thank you for making me so wonderfully complex!
Your workmanship is marvelous—how well I know it.*
PSALM 139:13–14 NLT

If you have
faith,
you don't have worry.

Imagine your life without worry.

Wouldn't you live more optimistically, confidently, and courageously? Not to mention all the time you would gain without needless worry cluttering your mind.

When you relinquish your worries and troubles to God, faith sets in and sets you free.

Be anxious for nothing, but in everything by prayer and supplication, with thanksgiving, let your requests be made known to God.
PHILIPPIANS 4:6

Trust in God's plan.
You have a purpose
beyond the present moment.

Believe.

What can turn our world upside-down and fill our hearts and minds with frustration is that our plan isn't always God's plan.

Know that God created each and every one of us with a unique purpose in mind. During times of doubt or uncertainty, trust in God's plan for you.

"For I know the plans I have for you," declares the Lord,
"plans to prosper you and not to harm you,
plans to give you hope and a future."

JEREMIAH 29:11 NIV

It's no small thing...

to have faith
to love unconditionally
to willingly forgive
to extend grace

It's not easy being human! Let's face it. To walk in faith, to endure in love, to readily forgive, and show grace on a daily basis can be a challenge. That's why we need one another; to remind us that we don't have to do this alone.

Trust in the LORD with all your heart.

PROVERBS 3:5

Having faith
means it isn't necessary
to have all the answers.

Imagine what life would be like if you had all the answers to life's questions. Do you really want to know the outcome of every moment, every joy, and every challenge?

Having faith in God and faith in yourself means trusting beyond explanation and logic. While faith is unseen, it can be felt in the heart—a safe and loving place. Let your faith rest there.

Now faith is the substance of things hoped for, the evidence of things not seen.

HEBREWS 11:1

Faith
means being
open to
life.

Being open to life means being open to meeting new people, exploring opportunities to learn and grow, and even taking the occasional risk. When you're invited to have lunch with a friend, learn a new skill, or travel to an unfamiliar place, do you say an enthusiastic yes? Or do you find excuses to say no?

Trust God enough to place your life in His hands. After all, He knows best.

Like
the
Seasons,

we are restored
and
made new again!

Winters can be hard on everything—from our spirits, to wildlife, to vegetation. Have faith! Each spring the earth warms, and all is made new again. Tiny seeds majestically blossom into exquisite, fragrant flowers. Sleepy caterpillars transform into magnificent butterflies. And our dormant hearts awaken and come alive to the sun's life-giving rays.

Isn't God amazing?

We, who with unveiled faces all reflect the Lord's glory,
are being transformed into his likeness with ever-increasing glory,
which comes from the Lord, who is the Spirit.
2 CORINTHIANS 3:18 NIV

What's your real address?

We fuss so much over our earthly homes,
paging through magazines in search of the
perfect décor, or just the right paint color.
What short-sighted vision we have!

Heaven is our real home.
The most glorious place of all.

We are citizens of heaven,
where the Lord Jesus Christ lives.
PHILIPPIANS 3:20 NLT

God's love for us never changes.

We change.

We change hairstyles, lifestyles,
friends, homes, and jobs;
yet through everything,
God's love for us is never changing.

It is steadfast and true.

*For the LORD your God
will be with you wherever you go.*

JOSHUA 1:9 NIV

Sometimes life hurts.

You reach for the broken pieces of your heart.
You want to make it whole. But you're not sure
how to put it back together again.

A loss of a loved one, a job, your health, or loss of a dream
can fill you with despair and uncertainty. Or maybe you're
feeling lonely or disappointed. While you should honor
your feelings and heartache, know that you are not alone.

God is with you, walking beside you. Take His hand.

But those who hope in the LORD will renew their strength.
They will soar on wings like eagles; they will run and
not grow weary, they will walk and not be faint.

ISAIAH 40:31 NIV

Let God
do for you
what you cannot
do for yourself.

Surrender. Rest in God.

Lay your head on His shoulder.
Let Him take your worries and troubles
away as His love and peace envelope you.
Draw from the well that will never run dry.
He will never forsake or abandon you.

Therefore with joy you will draw water
from the wells of salvation.

ISAIAH 12:3

When you feel weary, pray

Oh Lord, I give you my heart and all that burdens it. Fill me with Your power and strength. Sustain me with Your mercy and love. Surround me with Your grace and peace. And to You I give all the glory for rest and renewal, amen.

I can do all things through Christ who strengthens me.

PHILIPPIANS 4:13

love

What
do
you
fear?

commitment

failure

success

change

We all have fears. It's only natural. A fear of crossing paths
with a snake can feel very real to some people.

But it's often the unseen fears—felt deep down in the
heart—that can rob us of life-giving opportunities and can
affect our relationships with family and friends. You know
them…fears like being loved, making a commitment, not
knowing the future, fear of failure or even success.

Surrender your fears, seen and unseen, to God now! He's
got you in His hands and He won't let you go. Live in His
light and love, abundantly and joyfully!

Having
faith
means
letting go.

Trusting in the unknown has inspired countless people to move across the country for a new job or education, accept a marriage proposal, or even change a signature hairstyle. Sometimes having faith simply means letting go of a heart-held belief or being comfortable.

Yet for many individuals, giving up what is known for the unknown is painfully difficult. For the faithful, accepting change and opportunity is a time of growing in God's love and becoming all we are meant to be.

Are you willing to give up what is for what could be?

Forgiveness

will set you free.

Sometimes we lose faith in friends
and family because they've let us down.
Disappointment can weigh heavy on our heart.
Yet none of us are beyond fault. We're all
on this human journey together.

Why not give others the same compassion and
understanding you would give yourself?

Blessed are the little joys in life.

They have the power to keep us going when we don't think we can.

Freshly washed sheets, sunshine on a chilly day, a random act of kindness, a surprise visit from a favorite friend, a prayer uplifted on our behalf—all of these acts bless our lives in surprising ways.

Be on the lookout for small moments of grace.

Experience
faith in action.

And let yours be
restored.

When your faith is stumbling, there is no better way to lift your spirits than to give others reason to smile.

Surprise a friend with a bouquet from your garden. Read to a child. Compliment a stranger. Share your time and talents for a worthy cause.

Feel your faith (and your heart) grow!

No matter what
challenges come your way,
always remember

you
are
loved.

Do you realize how many people love
you, pray for you, and care about you?
Accept small acts of kindness as evidence
of God's boundless love. Hold on to that
love to keep your faith strong.

Believe
in
your
dreams.

Anything is possible!

What do you dream of:
Traveling the world?
Earning an education?
Having a family?
Starting your own company?
Developing a skill or talent?

Even if your dream is as small as a mustard seed,
it could grow into something extraordinary if you have faith
in yourself and in God.

*If you have faith as a mustard seed,
you will say to this mountain, "Move from here to there,"
and it will move; and nothing will be impossible for you.*

MATTHEW 17:20

Celebrate
your
amazing
gifts and talents.

If God created all the beauty and majesty
that resides on this extraordinary earth, imagine
the talents and abilities He placed inside of you!
And while many of those gifts and talents have
been revealed and put into action, there are
others yet waiting to flourish.

Ask God for revelation. For confidence.
Be open to learning. Walk a new path of
discovery and possibility. Celebrate your gifts
and give the glory to God.

shine

Your brilliance may show in the kindness
and compassion you give to a stranger,
or how you listen to a neighbor without
judgment. Your brilliance may show in the way
you raise your children, or in the way you give
without expectation. Your brilliance may show in
your vocation, or in the art you create.

Let your brilliance glow brightly with God's love.

*Let your light shine before men, that they may
see your good deeds and praise your Father in heaven.*

MATTHEW 5:16 NIV

May
grace and gladness
fill each day of
your life.

What an extraordinary gift life is!
Unwrap each day with all your heart.
Savor it! Let God's grace surround you
and fill you with peace and joy.

When you have
faith
in
others,
shout it out!

Help others grow in confidence
by giving them encouragement and
affirmation. Simple statements like
"I believe in you" and "I'm proud of you"
can make a world of difference in
someone's life. Inspire others with your
kind and positive sentiments.

P.S. God believes in you, He's proud of
you, and He has faith in you too!

With every
breath,
be
faithful!

Let faith flow through you tenderly
like the waters of a gentle river. Inhale love,
acceptance, and conviction; exhale
your fears, frustrations, and worries.

You are worthy of peace and happiness.

May we always know
how to make each other
Smile
and give each other
reason to hope.

My promise to you is real. To lend hope
and a smile whenever, wherever I can. And
when I can't be by your very side, listen for
me. I'm whispering in your ear, reassuring
you, "Have faith. Trust. Everything will be okay.
God's grace and love will sustain you."

Keep this
little book where
you will see it often...

May these pages be a testimony of my faith in
you, and the special place you hold in my heart.
Whenever you need a lift or simply need to be
reminded of God's love for you, pick up this book
and consider yourself hugged and loved!

With God all things are possible.

Remember to keep

a dream in your
heart
and
faith in your
pocket...
and
always

eat your peas!

A portion of the profits from the
Eat Your Peas Collection
will benefit empowerment programs
for both youth and adults.

About the author:

Cheryl Karpen believes with faith, anything is possible.
An effervescent speaker, she passionately
brings inspiration, insight, and humor to her audience.
To learn more about Cheryl speaking at
your next event, visit www.cherylkarpen.com
or contact her at T) 612-207-4875.

Why Peas?

She was a vibrant, dazzling young woman with a promising future.
Yet, at sixteen, her world felt sad and hopeless.

Though I was living over 1800 miles away, I wanted to let this very special young person in my life know that I would be there for her, across the miles and through the darkness. I wanted her to know she could call me any time, at any hour, and I would be there for her. And I wanted to give her a piece of my heart that she could take with her anywhere—a reminder that she was loved.

Really loved.

Her name is Maddy, and she was the inspiration for my first book in the Eat Your Peas series, Eat Your Peas for Young Adults. At the very beginning of her book, I made a place to write in my phone number so she would know I was serious about being available. And right beside the phone number, I put my promise to listen—truly listen—whenever that call came.

Soon after the book was published, people began to ask me if I had the same promise and affirmation for adults. It was then that I realized it isn't just young people who need to be reminded of how truly special they are. We all do.

Today, Maddy is thriving and giving hope to others in her life. I like to think that, in some way, my book and I were part of helping her achieve that. If someone has given you this book, it means you are a pretty amazing person to them, and they wanted to let you know. Take it to heart.

Believe it, and remind yourself often.

Wishing you peas and plenty of joy,

Cheryl Karpen

P.S. My mama always said, "Eat your peas! They're good for you." The pages of this book are filled with nutrients for your heart. They're simply good for you too!

Other books by Cheryl Karpen

The Eat Your Peas Collection™

is now available in the following titles:

Sisters
Daughters
Sons
Mothers
Grandkids
New Moms
Tough Times

Daughter-in-law
Birthdays
Someone Special
Girlfriends
Extraordinary
  Young Person

New titles are SPROUTING up all the time!

Heart and Soul Collection

To Let You Know I Care
Hope for a Hurting Heart
Can We Try Again? Finding a way back to love

For more inspiration, Like us on Facebook at the **Eat Your Peas Collection**.
For quotes and pretties to post, follow us on Pinterest at
www.pinterest.com/eatyourpeasbook/

To view a complete collection of our products, visit us online at www.eatyourpeas.com

Eat Your Peas® Faithfully

Unless otherwise noted, all scripture is taken from the NEW KING JAMES VERSION.
©1982, 1992 by Thomas Nelson, Inc. Used by permission.

Other scriptures are taken from the HOLY BIBLE: NEW INTERNATIONAL VERSION ® (NIV).
©1973, 1978, 1984 by International Bible Society.
Used by permission of Zondervan Publishing House. All rights reserved.
Holy Bible, New Living Translation (NLT). ©1996.
Used by permission of Tyndale House Publishers, Inc., Wheaton, Ill 60189.
All rights reserved.

ISBN-13: 978-0-9711794-5-5
Home grown in the USA

For more information, contact:
Gently Spoken
PO Box 365
St. Francis, MN 55070

Toll-free 1-877-224-7886 or visit us online at
www.eatyourpeas.com

Published by Gently Spoken